The smallest and the bravest

Chapter 1

The club hut was swaying madly. Everyone thought it would be fun to sleep outside for a night, but no one thought it would be such a stormy night.

The rain was lashing the windows and the wind was howling through the branches of the tree.

Ben looked out through the window. It was getting light, but everyone else in Sandy Bay would still be fast asleep.

How he wished that he was snuggly tucked up in his soft, warm bed in the house.

Rob, Ali and Kim were asleep in their sleeping bags, but Ben was frightened. He didn't like the tree and the club hut swaying so much.
He was very frightened!

Down below Ben could see Pen's big red tent, where Pen and Sue were sleeping. He thought they would be sound asleep, and wouldn't be pleased if he crept down the ladder to share their tent.

Anyway, he thought all the others would laugh at him, and say he was too scared to sleep in the hut for the whole night!

Chapter 2

"What was that?" shouted Ali as he shot out of his sleeping bag.
Rob and Kim went on sleeping.
They hadn't heard the loud crack.

"I think it was a branch cracking in the strong wind," said Ben, now really wishing that he was safely snuggled up in his soft, warm bed in the house. He looked over to the house, but all the curtains were still closed. He knew Mum and Dad wouldn't be awake for a long time yet!

“Wake up Rob, wake up!” shouted Ben.
“We think something has happened.
We think a branch has cracked.”

“Oh, go back to sleep Ben.
It’s only 5 o’clock and I’m really tired,”
grumbled Rob.

"There it was again," said Ali.

And just as he spoke the boys felt the hut give a sudden lurch!
All four went sliding across the floor!
"Ouch!" said Kim, "That hurt!"

The hut was still swaying in the strong wind. The boys carefully got to their feet.
The noise of the wind was getting louder.

“It’s the branch the hut is fixed to!”
shouted Kim, in a frightened voice.
“It has cracked and the hut is leaning
right over, and the ladder has gone!”

“We’re going to crash to the ground!” screamed Ben, above the wind.
“And look, we are hanging over the tent, where the girls are sleeping!” cried Rob.

Chapter 3

The storm was now making so much noise that the boys couldn't make the girls hear.

"We must wake them, before the hut crashes down on their tent!" cried Ben.

“Quick Ben, get the rope,” called Ali.
“I’ll try to climb onto the next branch, and then down the tree.”

“You can’t,” shouted Rob.
“You’re too heavy and the branch is too thin. It will break and you’ll fall.”

"I can," shouted Ben. "The branch is thin but I am small. I can climb out and it won't break."
"Are you sure?" said Ali, "We don't want you falling and hurting yourself."
"Yes, but I don't want my sister or Sue getting hurt!" said Ben.
"Well done," said Rob. "You may be small, but you're really brave, Ben!"

Chapter 4

Rob and Ali tied the rope round Ben's waist. The other end Kim tied to the tree.

"Now mind how you go!" shouted Rob above the roar of the wind, as Ben climbed along the branch.

Ben didn't dare look down. It was a long way! He had never liked being up high! He leaned over, carefully stretching to grab the next branch. The others watched, holding their breath and hoping their little friend wouldn't slip.

Then ... "Crack!"
Just as Ben grabbed it,
the branch gave way!
Ben felt himself going.
Rob and Ali and Kim watched.
They couldn't help now as Ben fell.
Down! Down! Down!

Ben suddenly stopped – just above the ground – the rope held ...

... and with a crash
he swung right under the hut,
and with a crunch,
right in the front of Pen's red tent.

"OUCH! What was that?" shouted Pen.
"Quick," shouted Ben.
"Come out here.
The branch is broken!
The hut might fall on you.
Get out here quickly, both of you."

"Ben might be the smallest and the youngest member of our gang, but he was the bravest last night," said Rob.

Ben felt really proud – and really pleased that he had not slept in his soft warm bed in the house!